Deposit Rate Advantages at the Largest Banks[*]

STEFAN JACEWITZ[†]   JONATHAN POGACH[†]

This Version: 21 February 2014

First Version: 16 November 2011

Abstract

We estimate differences in funding costs between the largest banks and the rest of the industry. Using deposit rates offered at the branch level, we eliminate many non-risk-related differences between banks. We document significant and persistent pricing advantages at the largest banks for comparable deposit products and deposit risk premiums. Between 2007 and 2008, the risk premium paid by the largest banks was 39 bps lower than the risk premium at other banks under the baseline estimate after controlling for common risk variables. These findings are consistent with an economically significant too-big-to-fail subsidy paid to the largest banks through lower risk premiums on uninsured deposits.

Keywords: *Too big to fail; Risk premium; Deposits; Interest rates*
JEL Codes: *G21, G28, H81*

Opinions expressed in this paper are those of the authors and not necessarily those of the FDIC

---

[*]The authors thank Carlos Arteta, William F. Bassett, Steve Burton, V. V. Chari, Bob DeYoung, Alireza Ebrahim, Ron Feldman, Levent Güntay, Robert Hauswald, Paul Kupiec, Myron Kwast, Oscar Mitnik, Don Morgan, George Pennacchi, Carlos Ramírez, Silvia Ramírez, Haluk Ünal, Skander Van den Heuvel, and Smith Williams, as well as participants in seminars at the Federal Reserve Board, the Federal Reserve Bank of Minneapolis, the University of Maryland, the Financial Management Association's 2012 annual meeting, the 2013 Banking Research Conference, the Research Task Force of the Basel Committee on Banking Supervision and China Banking Regulatory Commission, and the Center for Financial Research at the FDIC for their valuable comments and suggestions. Any remaining errors are the sole responsibility of the authors.

[†]Federal Deposit Insurance Corporation. Authors can be reached at sjacewitz@fdic.gov and jpogach@fdic.gov.

1 Introduction

This paper provides three pieces of evidence relating to the public discourse on the differential competitive environment enjoyed by the largest banks.[1] First, we show that the largest banks tend to offer lower interest rates on money market deposit accounts (MMDAs). Second, we show that the market demands a lower premium for risky products from the largest banks. Finally, we show that, even after controlling for common balance-sheet measures of risk, the largest banks receive a discount on risky deposits of approximately 39 bps relative to smaller banks. Our method and a battery of supporting tests rule out many common proposed explanations for this observed discount. Instead, the evidence is consistent with the explanation that the discount is a result of an implicit or perceived government support provided to "too-big-to-fail" (TBTF) institutions from 2007 to 2008.

Given the dominant role of deposits in funding both large and small banks, the analysis of potential pricing advantages based on bank size would be incomplete without a careful consideration of deposits. However, an examination of comparable deposit rate differences is currently absent from the literature. Instead, existing papers compare bond prices (e.g. Penas and Ünal (2004)), equity returns (e.g. Gandhi and Lustig (2010)), or CDS spreads (e.g. Schweikhard and Tsesmelidakis (2012)) between large and small banks. Yet deposits are by far the largest source of funds for banks, much larger than equity or bonds. Pre-crisis (year-end 2006) deposits represented 61% of total assets for banks larger than $200 billion and 68% for the rest of the industry.[2] Similar (though senior) to subordinated debt holders, uninsured depositors face a potential loss in the event of failure, and therefore should require less compensation for risk from a bank they feel will likely receive government support. This paper establishes a statistically and economically significant large-bank pricing advantage in

---

[1]Throughout the paper, *bank* refers to a depository institution (including thrifts) consolidated at the level of the regulatory high holder. In the baseline definition, we use $200 billion in assets as the large-bank threshold, though alternative thresholds are explored. See Subsection 3.1.

[2]Source: Call Report data

2

deposit rates and deposit risk premiums.

Importantly, some of the measured differences in the cost of funding cannot be attributed either to differences in common balance-sheet measures of risk or to many often cited non-risk-related factors, such as a convenient network of branch locations, additional services, alternative funding options, differences in loan opportunities, branding, and so forth. Like other researchers estimating a large-bank benefit, we cannot directly test a causal hypothesis that TBTF policies are the source of the differences. Still, a gap as large as 39 bps is evidence consistent with an economically significant TBTF subsidy paid to the largest banks.[3] We find a 39 bps large-bank deposit risk premium advantage in the baseline estimate before the 2008 financial crisis. Of course, any risk premium advantage should be present in all of the bank's funding sources. If these banks did receive such preferential risk pricing on all of their equity and uninsured liabilities, this advantage would have accounted for 27% of their 2007 aggregate pre-tax profits. Being senior to all of these other claims, a 39 bps advantage on uninsured deposits would likely imply an even larger overall advantage.

We exploit a largely unexplored data set (RateWatch) to add to existing papers that attempt to quantify a large-bank discount. Further, we examine differences in interest rates offered on MMDAs with a minimum deposit of $100K (hereafter, $100K MMDAs, and likewise for accounts with $25K and $10K deposit minimums) versus $25K MMDAs at a branch level. Using the within-branch differences to obtain a bank risk premium measure allows us to account for many non-risk factors that other studies neglect. Before the fourth quarter of 2008, the major difference between these two products (other than the minimum balance) was that one was entirely insured, and therefore riskless, while the other was only partially insured. The differencing approach then removes many important non-risk factors that are

---

[3]Observationally similar phenomena have been described variously as "too-systemically-important-to-fail" (Ueda and di Mauro (2012)), "too-complex-to-fail" (Herring (2002)), "too-difficult-to-fail-and-unwind" (Kane (2009)); and probably many others. For the purposes of this paper, we harbor no preference for one description over another. Here, we test for differences in deposit pricing based on size as measured by assets, though asset size is likely correlated with measures of systemic importance and complexity.

constant between these two deposit products within the same bank, leaving a more isolated measure of the risk premium.

We also exploit a statutory change to the insured deposit limit that lends additional support to the test for a large-bank risk premium advantage. Under the Emergency Economic Stabilization Act (EESA), passed in the fourth quarter of 2008, the insurance limit was raised to cover interest and principal up to \$250K, thereby encompassing the \$100K accounts used in our construction of the risk premium. Consistent with the interpretation that the differences between the largest banks' and other banks' measured risk premiums can be attributed to risk disparities, the difference decreased markedly as the \$100K MMDAs became insured. The fact that the change in the measured risk premium advantage for large banks was concurrent with this policy change substantially weakens many alternative non-risk explanations of the discount.

To establish a rate-level disparity, we examine differences in deposit interest rates between the largest banks and all other banks. We find that large banks pay a lower interest rate than other banks for comparable deposit products. In particular, we examine \$100K MMDAs between the first quarter of 2005 and the third quarter of 2010.[4] The interest rate offered by the largest banks on \$100K MMDAs was between 10 and 50 bps less than the rate offered by other banks. Since the government did not guarantee the interest on these deposits or principal over \$100K, any differences between banks in price will contain information on differences in perceived risk across institutions, possibly including expectations regarding TBTF policies.

While large banks paid less than smaller banks for \$100K MMDAs, on average, it is reasonable to suspect that this difference may be attributable to non-risk factors. Indeed, the largest banks paid 10 to 50 bps less than their smaller bank counterparts for \$25K MMDAs

---

[4]The particular analyses do not always use this full time span. Each subsection below gives in the text the beginning and end of the period used in the relevant analysis.

as well, despite the fact that the default risks associated with these deposits were identical, as the FDIC explicitly insures the entirety of these accounts for all banks up to the standard maximum deposit insurance amount (SMDIA). Therefore, this substantial difference must be attributable to any number of other factors, all of them unrelated to risk. That is, at least part of large banks' funding advantage is *not* related to TBTF considerations. For example, consumers may value the geographic footprint at a large bank and would be willing to receive a lower interest rate on their accounts, ceteris paribus. Alternatively, larger banks likely face a different competitive environment than smaller banks, which enables them to access funds at lower rates (see Park and Pennacchi (2009))). Either of these explanations forms an economies-of-scale type argument and demonstrates that bank funding costs may differ even when risk is held constant.

To isolate the risk premium, we examine the difference in interest rates offered for $100K MMDAs with rates offered for $25K MMDAs. Under an assumption that non-risk factors are constant between these two deposit products within the same bank, all that remains after differencing is the risk premium. In the absence of controls, we find that before the EESA, the risk premium paid by the largest banks was up to 45 bps less than that paid by smaller banks. However, even the difference in risk premiums need not be due to a TBTF subsidy. While it is true that bank risk affects the prices offered for deposit products, risk may indeed be lower at the largest banks without any government support. Many of these non-TBTF differences in risk should be measurable from banks' financial reports. Using common balance-sheet measures of risk, we reexamine the differences in banks' risk premiums. The remainder of the analysis examines whether the established difference in risk premiums is robust to a battery of different controls, specifications, and other alternative explanations.

We first run cross-sectional regressions to allow for a time varying risk premium gap. This analysis shows that the gap is statistically significant at a 90% level in five of the six quarters immediately preceding the failure of Lehman. The cross-sectional analysis also suggests that before 2007, risk at large banks was not priced much differently from risk at other banks in the data. Moreover, the cross-sectional analysis suggests that a $100 billion threshold is too low to find meaningful pricing discrepancies across banks. Rather, systematic price differences become more evident when the higher threshold of $200 billion (the baseline) is used. Under this specification, there are no banks in our sample between $200 billion and $500 billion before the crisis, so that this threshold is equivalent to a $500 billion threshold.[5] Nonetheless, we refer to this as a "$200 billion" threshold.

We then turn to a panel analysis to better exploit the time dimension of the data set. With the banks designated as large fixed at $200 billion, the baseline estimate of the risk premium gap between those banks and others is 39 bps and statistically significant before passage of EESA. In 2007, this discount translated to a $7.8 billion advantage for the largest banks on uninsured deposits alone. As a point of comparison, during 2007 these banks' aggregate net income before taxes was $102 billion, with aggregate interest expense of $146 billion. If the largest banks had enjoyed a 39 bps advantage across all uninsured liabilities and equity, this advantage would have been approximately $19 billion, or roughly 27% of their aggregate pre-tax profits. Given that $100K MMDAs are insured only up to the deposit minimum, these estimates reflect the risk premium from the perspective of partially insured accounts. Thus, the results presented here may be considered conservative estimates of the true risk premium gap.

In robustness analysis, we use the geographical richness of the data. In particular, large and small banks tend to operate in geographical markets that differ in potentially important ways. Therefore, one might expect that differences in $25K MMDA and $100K MMDA market characteristics across these regions could confound the baseline analysis. To address these concerns, we run our analysis aggregating bank quarters to the MSA level rather than

---

[5]This is in part a consequence of the absence of Washington Mutual and non-retail banks Bank of New York and State Street in the data. In addition, the baseline analysis excludes US Bancorp, as the bank posts a zero premium in every period in the data. See Section 5 for more details.

nationally and allow for MSA dummies. The magnitude of the large-bank pricing advantage remains statistically significant (at 49 bps) from 2007 to 2008 and drops to a 9 bps advantage after the increase in the SMDIA. As a further control on market area differences, for the five largest MSAs we restrict attention only to single metropolitan areas. We find that the results hold in four of the five largest areas (the lone exception is Chicago; we report only New York). Thus, accounting for geographic discrepancies between large and small banks does not eliminate our result.

The remainder of the paper is organized as follows: We review some of the existing literature and techniques for quantifying the TBTF premium in Section 2. Section 3 provides an overview of some important institutional information surrounding our estimation. Section 4 describes the empirical model and technique. Section 5 describes the data. We present the empirical results in Section 6 and conclude in Section 7.

2   Literature Review

In the existing literature, a variety of methods have been used to measure differences in size-related bank funding costs. The most straightforward way to compare the funding costs at large banks with the funding costs at other banks is to consider the average cost of funds (for examples, see Baker and McArthur (2009) and Li, Qu, and Zhang (2011); Acharya and Mora (2011) use the average cost of deposits). However, using the average cost of funds has a number of important limitations. First, it ignores differences in funding schemes across banks (e.g., access to wholesale markets or maturity structure). Second, banks may differ in funding costs for many reasons that a simple average inherently neglects (e.g., branch network and services). On the other hand, we use relatively standardized deposit products (MMDAs) and difference out many branch- and bank-specific non-risk factors to obtain and isolate a risk premium.

7

Another strand of literature measures TBTF by relying on credit agency ratings for banks. With this method, Acharya, Anginer, and Warburton (2013) estimate the funding cost advantage between 1990 and 2010 to be around 28 bps. Noss and Sowerbutts (2012), using a similar credit ratings approach, estimate the implicit subsidy to U.K. banks in 2009 to be in excess of $120 billion. In either of the preceding examples, the identification strategy relies entirely on credit rating agencies' proprietary and opaque determinations of both the targets and the extent of government support.

Alternatively, Hovakimian, Kane, and Laeven (2012) use market data to model the systemic risk benefit of a particular bank as that bank's contribution to a put option on the portfolio of aggregate bank assets. However, this technique is inherently backward looking, as it relies on the recent past of the volatility of stock returns to predict future volatility.

O'Hara and Shaw (1990) conduct an event study to estimate the value of the TBTF subsidy. They examine stock returns surrounding congressional testimony in 1984 from the Comptroller of the Currency in which he indicated that the eleven largest banks were subject to a TBTF policy. The authors show that following the testimony, abnormal stock returns were higher for the indicated banks than for other publicly traded banks. While that study has the cleanest causal mechanism, in the absence of a similar public statement around the time of the 2008 financial crisis, such an identification strategy is not possible for the recent period. Even so, that study can measure only the marginal effect of the announcement. If the market had already considered the largest banks to be TBTF, such an announcement would have had no effect.

Penas and Ünal (2004) study the large-bank discount using bond returns following merger announcements. They show that when the incremental change from the merger causes the bank to cross the 2% of industry assets threshold, the institution's bond returns decline about 15 bps more than do the returns for banks that do not cross this threshold. Similarly, Brewer and Jagtiani (2013) use data from 1991 to 2004 to look for the premium paid in the

8

eight mergers that brought the combined organizations over $100 billion in assets. They also perform an event study on abnormal stock returns following the announcement of such a merger and find in these mergers, acquiring firms paid a total premium of between $14 and $17 billion. Looking at equity prices following the passage of FDICIA, Kane (2000) uses a similar definition to show that, in "megamergers" between 1991 and 1998, the stocks of firms acquiring a large bank gained value as the size of the target institution increased.

Acharya and Mora (2011) consider the behavior of deposit rates during the crisis, including those at the largest banks. However, their data do not allow them to analyze comparable deposits across banks or possible non-risk-related determinants of deposit prices, as is done here. Moreover, deposit rate advantages at large banks is not the focus of their paper and is addressed only in passing.

Finally, our paper has strong parallels with Imai (2006), which studies weekly data of uninsured deposit rates of Japanese banks surrounding a 2002 drop in the deposit insurance limit. That study finds that weak banks exhibit outflows of uninsured depositors, even as they offer higher deposit rates. Furthermore, using a credit ratings approach as in Acharya, Anginer, and Warburton (2013), the Imai (2006) study finds that this kind of market discipline is weaker at banks subject to implicit guarantees. We use similarly constructed deposit rate data and a comparable change in the deposit insurance limit, though we focus on U.S. data and in the context is of the 2008 financial crisis.

3   Institutional Details

This section provides background for several elements of our estimation strategy; specifically, we define TBTF and describe MMDAs and the EESA.

3.1   Definition of "Too Big to Fail"

Being an *implicit* guarantee, a TBTF policy has no clear threshold. In reality, TBTF status is probably not a dichotomous variable defined around a threshold. Rather, an implicit TBTF subsidy would derive from a subjective expectation of the likelihood and extent of government support based on underlying variables such as size, complexity, and so forth. Thus, differences in any risk premium should go up gradually, as the market's estimate of the probability of being bailed-out goes to one. Nevertheless, a threshold of $100 billion in assets is commonly used as a proxy for these subjective expectations. However, Washington Mutual, a thrift with $307 billion in 2008, *did* fail. Moreover, Lehman Brothers, a $639 billion asset investment bank, failed in September 2008, even though the government had bailed out the considerably smaller Bear Stearns earlier that same year. Given these facts, it would be difficult to justify the claim that the market believed the government would rescue all banks over $100 billion in assets. Even ex post, the inconsistent use of bailouts makes a precise definition of a TBTF threshold impossible.

In this paper, we purposefully avoid taking a particular stance on the definition of a TBTF bank and focus instead on identifying a large-bank discount. We adopt several definitions previously established in the literature or by policy makers, often based on absolute or relative asset size. The baseline definition of a large bank uses a threshold of $200 billion in 2008 dollars, though we supplement the analysis with the more common $100 billion threshold. The $100 billion definition is derived from the Federal Reserve Board's requirement of additional supervisory review through the Supervisory Capital Assessment Program (SCAP) and later through the Comprehensive Capital Analysis and Review (CCAR) for all banks over $100 billion at the end of 2008, as described by Bernanke (2009). We include similar tests using a $10 billion threshold merely as a point of comparison, though these banks are generally not considered to be TBTF.

3.2 Description of Money Market Deposit Accounts

MMDAs are an important source of funding for commercial banks. At the 2005 start of the sample, MMDAs constituted approximately 23% of aggregate bank liabilities, a share they held until the financial crisis in 2008. Following the crisis, MMDAs increased to approximately 29% of total bank liabilities.[6] As most MMDAs are insured, this increase mimics a general trend since 2008 toward insured deposits.[7]

The differencing approach used to isolate the risk premium requires that the non-risk factors associated with $100K MMDAs and $25K MMDAs be sufficiently uniform. MMDAs are a type of savings deposit and therefore face a number of statutory restrictions that make them relatively homogenous across deposit minimums.[8] For all MMDAs, the depository institution may, at any time, require written notice of a withdrawal not less than seven days before the withdrawal. Moreover, like all savings accounts, MMDAs are allowed no more than six withdrawals or transfers per month. These restrictions on access are uniform across all banks and all MMDAs and therefore limit the differences in service between different MMDA accounts.

Though we are unable to directly test the degree of uniformity between products, there are reasons to believe it holds to some extent. First, the existence of higher thresholds for MMDA accounts (e.g., $250K) at many banks implies that the markets for accounts with $25K and $100K minimums reflect the marginal difference in deposit products. Importantly,

---

[6]Source: FDIC.

[7]MMDAs are often the targets of swept accounts. These are an important type of account that should be (but often is not) accounted for in most analyses using MMDAs, but has no impact on this study in particular. Banks routinely sweep funds from checking accounts into MMDAs at the end of business days and back again before the start of the next business day, typically without the depositor's knowledge. The purpose of these sweeps is often to reduce banks' reserve requirements, as the reserves required on savings accounts are zero and positive for checking accounts. By creating these sweep account, banks can decrease their reserve requirement by up to 70% (see Anderson and Rasche (2001) and VanHoose and Humphrey (2001)). This type of MMDA represents some $800 billion (Source: Federal Reserve Bank of St. Louis) in the total value of savings accounts, but pays no interest. It is important to understand that these types of MMDAs are not applicable to this study, do not show up in the data, and are not a source of competition with retail MMDAs.

[8]See 12 CFR §204.2(d)(2); Reg. D, 45 FR 56018, Aug. 22, 1980.

these minimums are relatively close; we are not comparing the markets for $10,000 accounts with those for $1,000,000 accounts. Second, within the range of deposit sizes that we consider, there is evidence of only modest differences across markets. For example, Kennickell, Kwast, and Starr-McCluer (1996) estimate that a decrease in the deposit insurance limit from $100K to $25K would not be associated with a dramatic change in many non-wealth household characteristics. Third, if there were systematic differences in the $25K MMDA and the $100K MMDA depositor preferences or characteristics, one would expect these differences to be relatively persistent over time (for example, differences in financial sophistication or the valuation of large branch networks should change very slowly). Consequently, if our results were driven by a violation of this assumption, we would not expect to see marked rapid changes in the estimates over time. However, the results show that differences in the risk premium paid by large banks quickly vanished following passage of the EESA.

3.3   Description of the Emergency Economic Stabilization Act

A statutory change allows further examination of how well the risk premium measure incorporates a risk premium. Further, the results from this examination weaken many non-risk-related interpretations of the measured large-bank discount before the crisis. On October 3, 2008, amidst the financial crisis and mounting numbers of bank failures, President George W. Bush signed the Emergency Economic Stabilization Act into law, which increased the SMDIA covered by the FDIC to $250K. Initially, the increase in SMDIA was set to expire on December 31, 2009. However, subsequent legislation extended the increase, ultimately made the increase permanent and retroactive to January 1, 2008 under the Dodd-Frank Wall Street Reform and Consumer Protection Act signed into law by President Barack Obama.

The data include periods in which the $100K MMDAs are only partially insured and periods after the crisis when they became fully insured (temporarily, retroactively, or permanently, depending on the concurrent information). We support the validity of our overall approach and conclusions by examining the changes around the passage of the EESA. As the Act resulted in equivalent insurance for $25K and $100K MMDAs, we would expect the differences across banks to decrease or even disappear. This is, indeed, exactly what we found, as reported in Section 6. However, because of the incremental way in which the increase in the SMDIA became permanent, and given the widespread market disruptions during the crisis, this robustness test should be interpreted cautiously.[9]

4   Model

A major difference between the explicit interest rate that a bank pays on $25K MMDAs, denoted r, and the rate that it pays on $100K MMDAs, denoted R, is that the depositor is entirely insured for the former product but not for the latter product (before fourth quarter 2008). Consequently, $p = R - r$ represents a measure of the risk premium for a given bank.[10]

Our method constitutes a type of difference-in-difference technique (first across product, then across size, rather than across time, as the typical difference-in-difference approach). We will define a large-bank discount on the risk premium as

$$p_{small} - p_{large} = (R_{small} - r_{small}) - (R_{large} - r_{large}),$$

where p_{large} indicates the average risk premium for large banks, equivalent to the difference between R_{large} (the average rate offered for $100K MMDAs by large banks) and r_{large} (the average rate offered for $25K MMDAs by large banks). Subscript *small* variables are defined similarly for smaller banks.

An important benefit of using this technique is that it allows two dimensions of flexibility

---

[9]For example, if there are costs to switching banks, then a change in the SMDIA that was only temporary might not be sufficient to eliminate differences in risk premiums between large banks and other banks.

[10]The value p may also incorporate some level of liquidity risk. Even so, we expect liquidity risk to be minimal, given the degree of accessibility to funds in a MMDA. See the discussion in Section 3.2. Nevertheless, in all analyses we control for liquidity risk.

in the underlying assumptions.[11] In particular, the analysis holds as long as *either* of the following two conditions holds: First, the error in the measurement of risk premiums using the difference between products does not differ between the largest banks and other banks in a systematic way. Second, other non-risk elements of price related to being large do not differ in a systematic way across deposit products. To the extent that *both* of these conditions are simultaneously violated in a meaningful way, we will not have accurately measured the large-bank discount. Even so, robustness checks in Section 6 allow these assumptions to be somewhat relaxed. Further, to imply that there is no significant large-bank discount, the double violation of these assumptions would have to be such that small banks' risk premiums are inflated relative to large banks' risk premiums.

For example, suppose that there were differences in financial sophistication between $25K and $100K depositors.[12] In that case, the measure of bank-specific risk premiums would be inaccurate. However, so long as the same difference in financial sophistication between insured and uninsured depositors existed in large and small banks, the measurement of the large-bank discount would hold. Similar arguments can be applied to many other partial violations (e.g., differences in market competition or in funding preferences between large banks and others).

For the measure of the risk premium, p, to be meaningful, depositors in $25K and $100K MMDAs must truly face disparate levels of risk. The $25K MMDAs were under the SMDIA and were therefore explicitly guaranteed through the full span of the data. Insured deposits are backed by the full faith and credit of the United States. On the other hand, any principal and interest in excess of the SMDIA carries no explicit guarantee.

In addition to the legal distinction between insured and uninsured deposits, uninsured

---

[11]Examining the differences surrounding the policy change adds a third level of flexibility (similar to a difference-in-difference-in-difference technique). However, in that case, it is important to note that there are confounding factors that limit the interpretability.

[12]There is empirical evidence that this is not the case (as discussed in Subsection 3.2), however this supposition acts a useful illustrative tool.

deposits are exposed to real losses in practice. From the beginning of 2007 until the end of 2011, uninsured depositors saw losses at 32 banks. Nominal recovery rates at these banks averaged 33% as of the end of 2011.[13]

However, the franchise value generated from deposits implies that they are generally treated more favorably in a failure than other forms of debt, even conditional on the hierarchy of claims. For this reason among others, acquiring banks will often assume many or all of a failing bank's uninsured deposits in addition to insured deposits. Through this resolution mechanism, the market may then independently "insure" the uninsured deposits of large banks by assuming them in the event of failure. Despite this possibility, uninsured depositors took losses even at some of the larger bank failures during the recent crisis. The largest such bank was IndyMac, a $31 billion bank and the fourth largest bank failure in history, at which uninsured depositors were expected to see only a 50% recovery of uninsured deposits.[14] It should also be noted that even when uninsured depositors are repaid in full in nominal terms, the repayment process may take years, while their insured counterparts have immediate and full access to funds in the event of failure.

4.1 Cross-Sectional Analysis

The model accounts for the risk premium p by looking at standard risk variables (X_{it} for bank i at time t) and determining whether being particularly large provides additional explanatory power on risk premiums. In the baseline model, the risk variables are the equity-asset ratio, merger-adjusted asset growth rate[15], nonperforming loans-to-assets ratio, loan loss reserves-to-assets ratio, non-brokered insured deposits-to-assets ratio, liquid assets-to-assets ratio,

---

[13]Source: FDIC.

[14]In unreported analysis, we find that conditional on failure, there is no systematic relationship between size and the probability that uninsured depositors face losses. Consequently, it is unlikely that the results given here are driven by differential treatment of uninsured depositors across bank size in the event of failure.

[15]There are a number of extreme values observed for asset growth. Thus, asset growth rates are Windsorized to a floor of -50% and a ceiling of 100%.

trading assets plus trading liability-to-assets ratio, income before taxes-to-assets ratio, and growth volatility (see Table 1 for details). These variables are intended to capture, to varying extents, each of the CAMELS[16] components. We also control for potential difference in the liquidity premium or behavioral pricing rules by including the difference between the $25K MMDA rate and the $10K MMDA rate. We examine the following model cross-sectionally at each point in time: for a fixed t, let

$$p_{it} = \beta_t X_{it} + \gamma_t Large_{it} + \varepsilon_{it}, \tag{1}$$

where ε_{it} is the error term and we allow parameters to vary over time, including the large-bank discount γ.

We run the regressions using alternative specifications for a large-bank threshold, namely, $10 billion, $100 billion, and $200 billion in 2008 dollars. The first serves as a point of comparison and control, rather than as a threshold that we believe to be relevant with regard to implicit government support. A list of U.S.-owned banks meeting the $200 billion and $100 billion criteria can be found in Table 2.

We purposely excluded from the baseline analysis one variable commonly associated with risk: size. A simple diversification argument suggests that given a level of loan risk, a larger bank with a single portfolio would face less volatility than a similar smaller bank, even in the absence of any external benefits that a bank may accrue from being very large. However, in such a context, size acts merely as a proxy for other measures of risk that should be observable in a bank's financial statements. For example, diversification benefits should be observable in lower asset volatility, or improved risk management should be manifest in lower charge-off rates (the analysis accounts for both of these risk metrics). Thus, if diversification

---

[16]Under the unified supervisory regime instituted by FDICIA, banks are evaluated according to six components of safety and soundness. Each letter in "CAMELSŠŠ refers to one of these components: Capital adequacy, Asset quality, Management, Earnings, Liquidity, and Sensitivity to market risk.

were responsible for the result, it would have to materialize in a manner not captured by the other controls. Meanwhile, including size as a regressor in addition to *Large* introduces an obvious multicollinearity problem. Still, *size* (log assets) is included as an alternative regressor to the *Large* dummy as a further robustness test. Results from this test, discussed in Subsection 6.3, suggest that this is not the force driving the result.

4.2   Panel Analysis

For the panel analysis, we split the sample into two periods: a pre-EESA sample and a post-EESA sample. In the pre-EESA sample p_{it} is expected to incorporate risk, given that the $100K MMDA accounts are not fully insured. In the post-EESA sample, both types of accounts are equally insured and so p_{it} is not expected to reflect any differences in risk. However, this expectation is tempered by the fact that the increase in the SMDIA was not made permanent until late in the post-EESA sample, and therefore p_{it} could feasibly still reflect some residual risk.

Consider a panel version of the model:

$$p_{it} = \alpha_t + \beta X_{it} + \gamma Large_i + \eta_i + \epsilon_{it}, \tag{2}$$

where α_t captures time fixed effects, η_i captures bank fixed effects, and ϵ_{it} is the error term. Assume that γ and β are constant over time to give the panel model some power relative to the cross-sectional specification. Furthermore, *Large* is fixed over time in the panel analysis and is a dummy defined using the mean asset observed for each sample (pre- and post-EESA). This is done to prevent the estimation of γ from being determined using within-variation of banks moving from below to above the threshold. That is, in the case that *Large* were time variant, γ would be estimated by looking at banks that cross the admittedly arbitrary threshold, while systematic differences between the very largest banks and others would be

17

ignored.

However, fixing $Large_i$ over time and including fixed effects η_i in the textbook fashion introduces a collinearity problem so that η_i and γ cannot be estimated together. Following Polachek and Kim (1994), Oaxaca and Geisler (2003), and Krishnakumar (2006), we further examine the unexplained remainder by regressing the estimated fixed effects from the within estimate on the $Large_i$ variable. The first stage gives predicted values of $p_{it} - \hat{\beta}X_{it} = \gamma Large_i + \eta_i + \epsilon_{it}$. Taking the individual bank mean of these estimated errors across time provides the estimated (time-invariant) bank-level fixed effects. The parameter estimates may then be interpreted as the mean difference between "large" and other banks in the residual risk premium that is unexplained by balance-sheet risk measures or branch-specific differences. In alternative specifications, we also estimate the $Large$ dummy using a pooled panel analysis and a random effects analysis.

5 Data

We use RateWatch data of branch-level deposit product prices.[17] Customer banks request competitor pricing data from RateWatch based on a particular market area. In assembling the data, RateWatch surveys target banks on the rates offered on various deposit products at the branch level. RateWatch describes the process by which it obtains the data as follows:

> RateWatch works with institutions to determine the schedule upon which rates/fees
> are updated. For deposit information, RateWatch tracks the day of the week
> rates are reviewed and obtains the rate information on or after that day, prior
> to a report's scheduled delivery. Market Research Specialists also verify the last
> change date when calling contacts and the effective dates of faxes, emails, and

---

[17]To the best of our knowledge, the only other paper using this data set is Ben-David, Palvia, and Spatt (2011), who show that poorly capitalized banks actually paid lower deposit rates on CDs in 2009-2010.

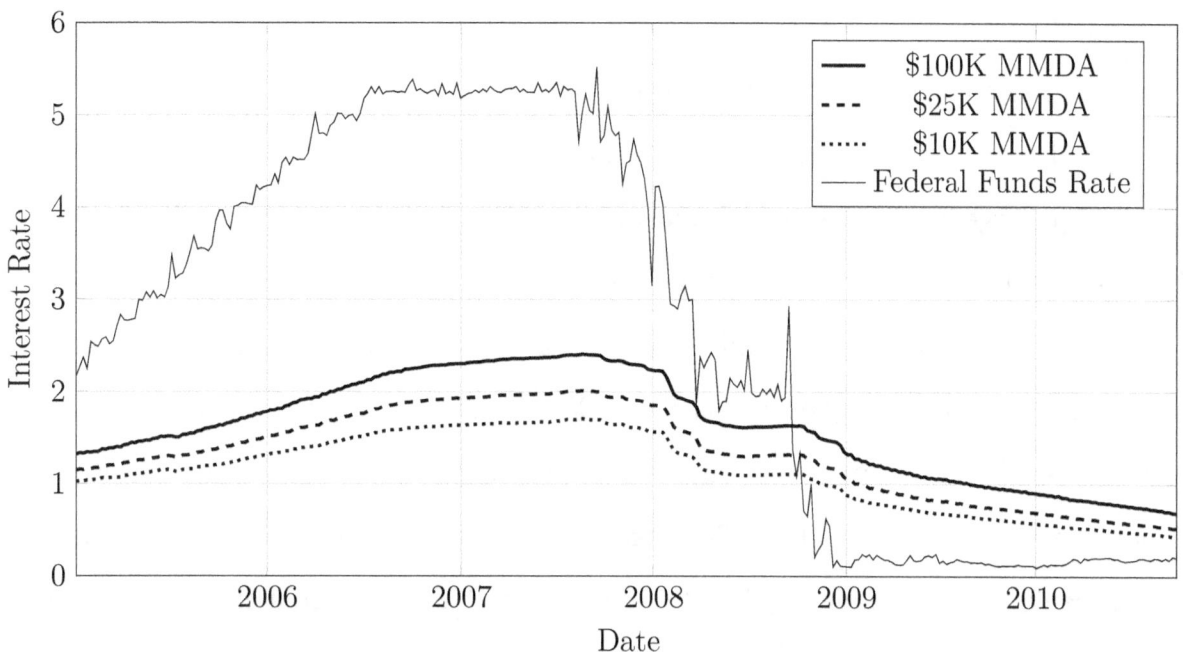

Figure 1: Mean interest rates. This figure gives the average interest rate paid on MMDAs with various minimum balances on a branch-by-branch basis from the beginning of 2005 until the third quarter of 2010. The effective Federal Funds rate is also given purely as a frame of reference (source: Board of Governors of the Federal Reserve System).

websites.[18]

The cross-sectional analysis runs from the first quarter of 2005 until the third quarter of 2010 for MMDAs with deposit minimums of $10K, $25K, and $100K. The mean MMDA rates from the RateWatch data are reported in Figure 1. The MMDA interest rates can be seen to broadly follow the movement of the effective fed funds rate, though the deposit interest rates are generally more stable.

Bank-level risk premiums for each quarter are obtained through a unit-weighted average across branches.[19] However, many banks do not post a $100K rate in the data, posting rates only for deposit products with lower minimums. As a result, bank coverage is more limited,

---

[18]http://www.rate-watch.com/faq.

[19]Weighting by deposits produces similar estimates for nearly all banks. For those banks where it makes a difference, the result is driven by branches offering deposit rates but recording no deposits in the Summary of Deposits data. Banks offering deposit rates yet seemingly holding no deposits may be the consequence of consolidated deposit recording across multiple branches in the SOD data.

especially early in the sample.

Figure 2 gives the number of current branch-level observations. The secular increase in the number of branches reflects the increasing number of banks participating in the survey. The data set is large in terms of bank branch observations, steadily increasing from around 35 thousand at the beginning of the sample to around 55 thousand by the end. The same figure also provides the total number of individual banks appearing in the data. The sample represents 14% of all banks in the first quarter of 2005 up to 38% in the third quarter of 2010. However, the data contain almost all large banks and therefore covers the vast majority of total industry assets, 71% at year-end 2007. Coinciding with an increase in the SMDIA, the number of banks increases from 1,695 to 2,178 from the third to the fourth quarter of 2008. Otherwise, the increase in the number of banks observed in the data is fairly steady. Lastly, we include only domestically owned (U.S.) banks. Looking only at banks that file a Call Report and for which a risk premium can be calculated leaves us with 22,224 bank-quarter observations over 12 quarters used in the baseline sample period.[20]

Ultimately, the goal is to connect empirically a bank's risk premium with measures of that bank's level of risk. Therefore, we use balance-sheet measures of risk from the Call Reports produced by all banks at the end of each quarter. First, we use the regulatory high holder as the appropriate decision-making entity, rather than the individual bank by charter. We do this since we expect large-bank benefits (including any possible TBTF subsidy) to apply at the highest level of organization.

We restrict attention to the last deposit rate observation for each branch-quarter to relate to the balance-sheet data. For 99% (73%) of branch-quarter observations, the most recent observed deposit rate was within the previous two (one) weeks of the quarter end.[21] We then link these branch-quarter observations to the regulatory high holder and calculate the

---

[20]See Table 2 for a list of the large banks that are found in the data.

[21]We also run the analysis using only deposit rate data from within a week of the quarter end, and the (unreported) results are quantitatively similar.

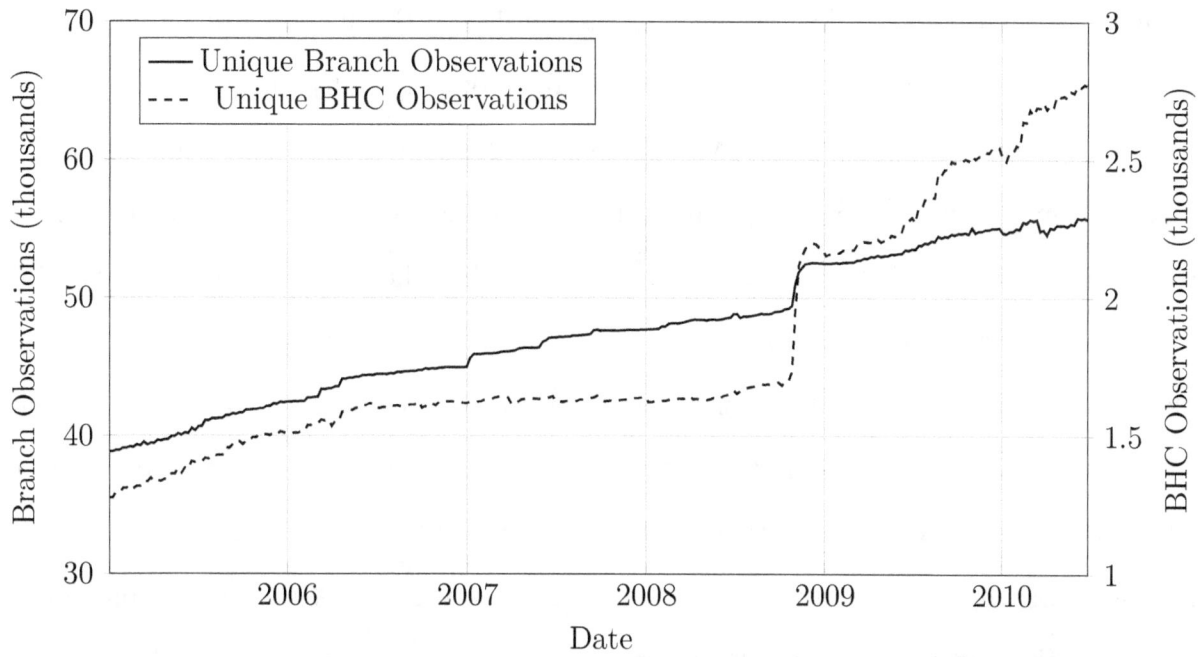

Figure 2: Daily Number of Branch and Quarterly Bank Observations. This figure gives the total number banks and branches that are actively reporting interest rates. That is, the bank branch reported 10K, 25K, and 100K MMDA rates *before and after* a given date.

average risk premium (the $100K rate less the $25K rate) for each bank-quarter across all branches. For any given bank, the risk premiums do not vary significantly across branches within a state but may vary markedly across states.[22]

Table 3 reports sample statistics for the variables across all quarters used in the baseline panel analysis.[23] This table can be used to compare the risk characteristics of large versus other banks. It shows that with the exception of trading assets, the distributions of the control variables have largely overlapping support across large and other banks. The median bank in the sample has assets of $330 million (in 2010 dollars). This suggests that the sample over-represents large banks, as this is more than twice the asset size of the median bank observed for the same sample period in the population of banks. The equity-asset ratio, nonperforming loans-asset ratio, loan loss reserves-asset ratio, and merger-adjusted growth

---

[22]This is consistent with Heitfield and Sabarwal (2004) and Park and Pennacchi (2009), among others.

[23]A list of the variable abbreviations can be found in Table 1.

all have significant outliers. Still, we include these outliers in the analysis, though unreported robustness checks showed that excluding them did not materially affect the results. As expected, the average and median MMDA rate is increasing with the minimum deposit.

Approximately one-third of bank-quarter observations have identical $25K and $100K rates every period, implying a risk premium of zero. For the 3,138 banks in the baseline sample period, 929 always report a zero risk premium, 1,640 always report a strictly positive risk premium, and 569 report a mix of zero and strictly positive risk premiums. In the baseline analysis, we include only those banks that post a strictly positive risk premium in at least one period. We assume that banks that *never* differentially price their products must use a pricing rule that ignores the market's perceived risk of the institution. Those institutions that differentially price their products in *at least one* period are assumed to have a risk premium that conveys at least some information on the perceived risk of the institution and so are included in the baseline regression. As a robustness check, we run the analysis using all bank-quarter observations and obtain similar, if somewhat attenuated, results.

6   Results

The results are broken down into three parts. First, we show that large banks pay less for comparable products. Second, we show that large banks pay a lower risk premium than other banks. While the first two results are descriptive in nature, establishing these as stylized facts is important to the discourse surrounding pricing advantages at the largest banks. Third, we show that this difference in risk premiums cannot be attributed to usual balance-sheet measures of risk.

6.1 Levels

Figures 3 and 4 show the evolution of MMDA rates over time for large banks and smaller banks, along with the differences in means for each group over time. The trends for the $25K and $100K MMDAs are similar, rising until the second quarter of 2007 before falling to the sample minimums by the third quarter of 2010. As expected, however, the rates for the $100K accounts are generally higher than the rates for the $25K accounts.

Furthermore, it is important to note that there are systematic differences in $25K MMDA rates between the large banks and smaller banks. This is the case even though $25K deposits are explicitly insured for all banks, regardless of size or systemic importance. This difference suggests that at least some of the large-bank funding advantages emanate from factors unrelated to implicit government guarantees. That is, this rate difference in identical riskless products may suggest that depositors extract non-pecuniary benefits from banking with a larger institution or that larger banks have access to other, cheaper funds. Moreover, this riskless deposit advantage along with the fact that large banks rely relatively less on retail insured deposits suggests that large banks' funding advantages may be even greater for uninsured funds.

Focusing on the difference between the $100K and $25K MMDA rates isolates the risk premiums, separating them from premiums paid for other potential benefits of being large (e.g., a larger branch network, a broader array of services).[24] It seems reasonable to assume that non-risk-related benefits from size are at least approximately equal across $25K and $100K MMDAs. To the extent that this is true, the difference in rates represents a measure of the risk premium paid by banks to attract funds into relatively risky deposit products. The differences in the risk premiums paid by the largest banks and other banks for uninsured

---

[24]Using the difference between the $100K and the $10K MMDA rates provides another measure of the risk premiums. However, whatever non-risk-related differences exist between products would be less pronounced between $100K and $25K MMDAs because of their closer deposit minimums. Thus, these products provide a better measure of risk premiums. Nevertheless, applying the same analysis as given below except exchanging the $10K for the $25K.

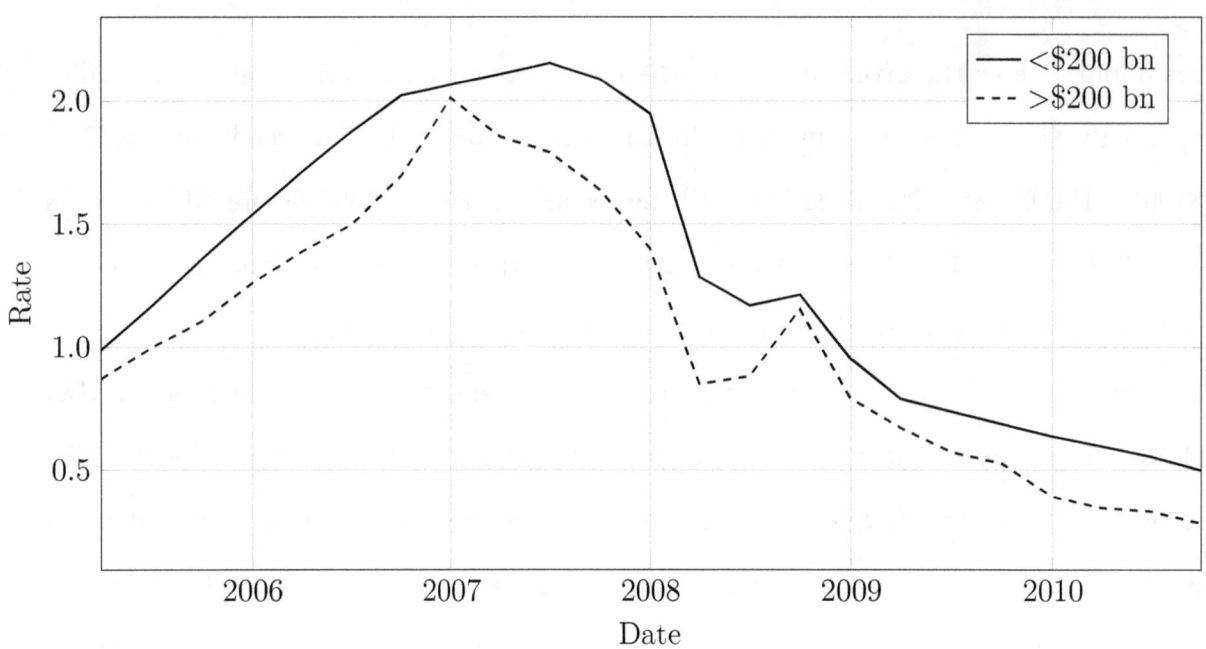

Figure 3: Mean Interest Rates on 25K MMDAs for Large and Other Banks.

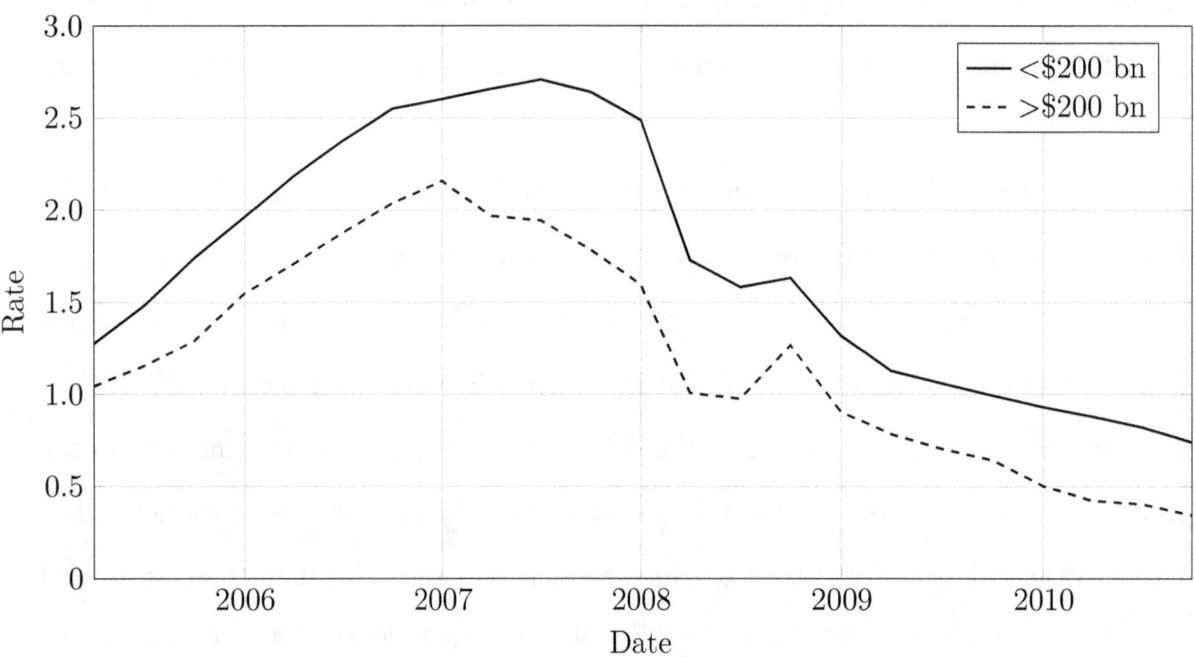

Figure 4: Mean Interest Rates on 100K MMDAs.

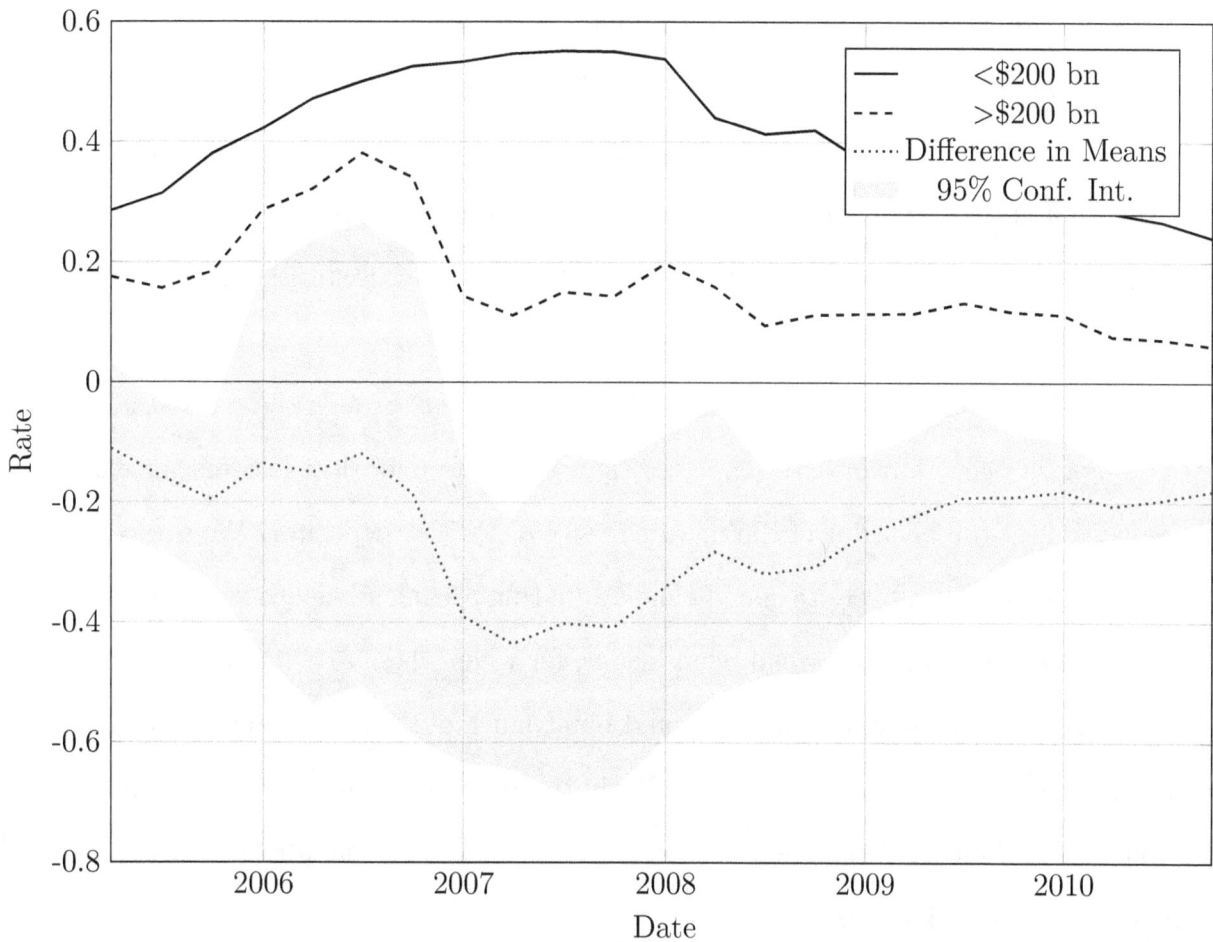

Figure 5: Mean Premium on $100K MMDAs for Large and Other Banks, and the Difference. That is, the difference between the riskless $25K MMDAs and the risky $100K MMDAs. The shaded region represents the 95% confidence interval around the difference in means.

deposits are shown in Figure 5. The average risk premium discount received by the largest banks rises to approximately 45 bps during 2007 before falling to about 20 bps at the end of the sample.

6.2 Risk Premium (Cross-Sectional)

First we run cross-sectional regressions to test for differences in the risk premium paid, after accounting for other risk variables, as in Equation 1. Table 4 reports the coefficients on the *Large* term over the sample. The baseline analysis aggregates banks to the regulatory high holder across all branches, though we obtain similar results when aggregating banks at the MSA level and running regressions with MSA fixed effects.[25] Under the baseline specification, after controlling for common balance-sheet risk variables from 2007 through the increase in the SMDIA, we find that large banks pay a notably lower risk premium. Even with only five banks over \$200 billion in the sample before the crisis, this difference is statistically significant for three-quarters of 2007 at 5% significance or more.

The other risk variables in the analysis are often insignificant through the cross-sectional analysis, though they generally have the expected sign. One reason for their insignificance may be that prices reflect the behavior of the marginal \$100K MMDA depositor. We conjecture that such a depositor is less likely to spend time evaluating a bank's balance sheet to assess the bank's riskiness than is the marginal bond-holder, for whom these risk variables are likely to be more evident. If this were the case, it would blunt much of the significance of the usual risk variables. On the other hand, bank size is likely to be salient to all market participants. In addition, multicollinearity may be a problem with regard to the significance of the risk variables in the cross-sectional analysis.

In Figure 6we compare alternative thresholds: \$200 billion, \$100 billion, and \$10 billion. The \$10 billion threshold is used as a point of comparison with large banks that are not thought to be subject to implicit government support. Although significance levels are not explicitly provided in the figure, standard errors for the \$200 billion threshold are provided in Table 4; other thresholds are typically insignificant. There are four other important points about Figure 6.

First and foremost, the large-bank discount for banks above \$200 billion is high from mid-2006 until the crisis but vanishes entirely after fall 2008, coinciding with the increase in SMDIA. The drop in the risk premium begins in the fall of 2008, consistent with the

---

[25]MSA-level results for the panel analysis are reported below. However, cross-sectional results are left unreported.

interpretation that differences in the measured risk premiums were indeed the product of differences in perceived risk between large banks and other banks. Given the chaotic financial and regulatory environment at that time, it is difficult to test directly the role of the EESA in reducing the measured large-bank risk premium advantage. Nevertheless, the reduction in the estimated large-bank advantage during that time rules out many non-risk-related explanations for the measured premiums in 2007.

The second and related point is that the banks larger than the $10 billion and $100 billion cutoffs have systematic price differences from smaller banks, but these differences are unchanged under the increase in SMDIA in fall 2008. This holds despite the fact that $10 billion banks are clearly not TBTF. However, as opposed to the $200 billion threshold, the difference between banks above and below $10 billion is largely unrelated to risk, as this premium remains unchanged despite equal insurance following the increase in SMDIA.

Third, there is little evidence of differences in prices across any threshold before 2007. This result is consistent with the findings of Acharya, Anginer, and Warburton (2013) and Hovakimian, Kane, and Laeven (2012). In both studies, there is no evidence of a significant risk premium before 2006 or 2007. From the perspective of bank deposits, the absence of a risk premium occurs during a time when there were zero bank failures (2005-2006) and little sign of bank stress to come.

Finally, the price differentials are most apparent at the $200 billion threshold, and they are notable at the $100 billion threshold only because of the influence of the banks greater than $200 billion. If the latter banks are excluded, there is no notable difference between $10 billion and $100 billion risk premiums.

6.3   Risk Premium (Panel)

Tables 5 and 6 report the results from the panel estimation along with nineteen alternative specifications. Unless otherwise noted, each sample considers the period of first quarter 2007

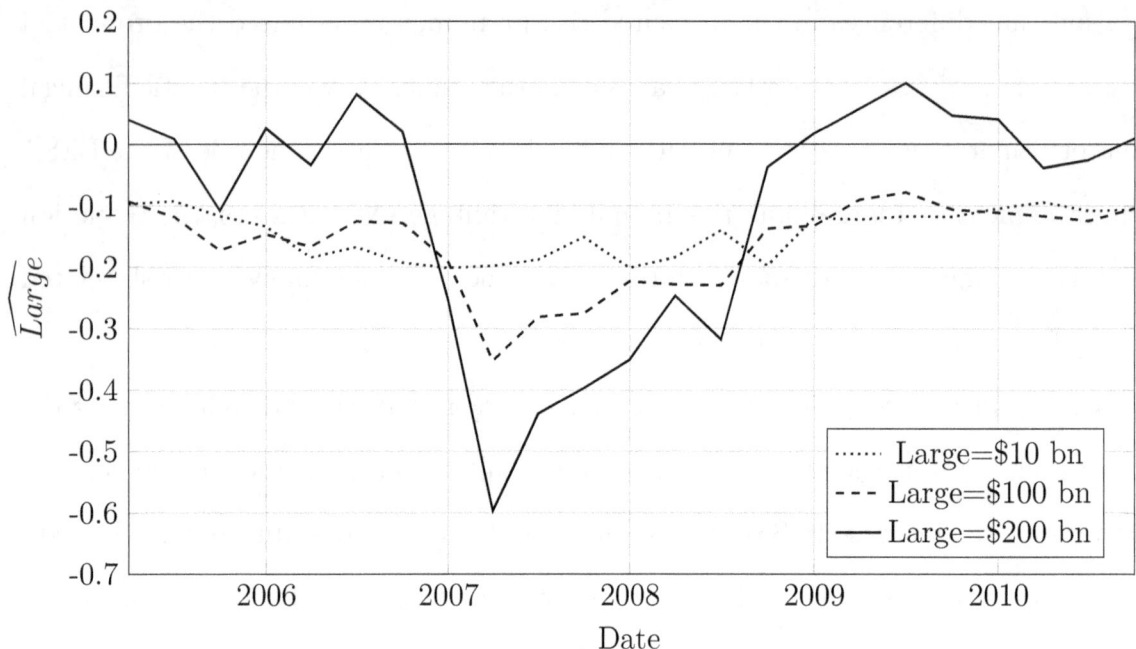

Figure 6: Cross-Sectional Estimated *Large* Dummy Parameter under Different Thresholds.

until second quarter 2008. This time span is based on the periods in which the cross-sectional analysis indicated a significant risk premium advantage. In the baseline analysis, we use a fixed effects method, a $200 billion threshold based on the cross-sectional analysis results, excluding those banks that post a zero premium in every quarter of the sample, and clustering errors at the bank level where appropriate. After controlling for common balance-sheet risk measures, we estimate a large-bank discount (that is, the mean difference in the unexplained risk premium differences between "large" and other banks) of approximately 39 basis points, which is significant at the 1% level. This number reflects the systematic risk pricing benefit obtained by these few largest banks that is not explained by the other measures of risk. This result is consistent with the hypothesis that these banks benefit from implicit (or perceived) government support. However, the analysis, like that of nearly every other paper in the literature, does not allow us to eliminate *all other* potential sources of the price discrepancy between large banks and other banks.

To examine alternative interpretations of the results, we consider a number of other specifications. In column (2), we apply the baseline analysis to the period after passage of the EESA; fourth quarter 2008 to third quarter 2010. Under our interpretation of the large-bank discount as resulting from perceived differences in risk, the increase in the SMDIA eliminates any inter-bank differences in risk for $100K MMDA accounts, as all become explicitly insured. The results show that after the increase in the SMDIA, the large-bank discount notably drops by 35 bps and is not statistically different from zero. We run a similar analysis estimating a large-bank pricing advantage using pooled and random effects methods. Comparable to the fixed effects approach, the pooled estimate of the large-bank premium reported in column (3) is 40 bps leading up to the crisis and drops to 0 bps after passage of the EESA, reported in column (4). Using a random effects estimator, we obtain similar estimates for the baseline sample period (43 bps, column (5)) and after the increase in SMDIA (-2 bps, column (6)).

As noted in Section 5, the set of banks in the data increases concurrently with the increase in SMDIA. Such an increase reflects either an increase in the number of banks whose pricing information is requested by their competitors or an increase in the number of banks offering rates for the $100K MMDA product. In either case, we perform additional tests to ensure that our pre- and post-EESA comparison is not driven by this compositional change. In particular, we run the analysis while fixing the set of banks to those that are in the data as of March 31, 2007; columns (7) and (8) show the results. The magnitude of the pre-EESA estimate remains largely unchanged, though the post-EESA estimate increases to 19 bps. Nevertheless, the pre- to post-EESA drop-off remains large and demonstrates that the results are not simply a consequence of compositional changes in the data.

It would be reasonable to suspect that some of the differences in risk premium between the largest banks and smaller banks may be attributable to the different markets in which these banks operate. Indeed, larger banks tend to operate in larger markets, and vice versa for smaller banks. To account for this possibility, we exploit the geographical characteristics of the data, aggregating bank risk premiums to the MSA level rather than nationally. We then perform the identical analysis, except allowing for MSA fixed effects. Table 5 reports results for the pre- and post-EESA in columns (9) and (10), respectively. Relative to the baseline, estimates in both the baseline sample period and the post-increase in the SMDIA period increase by about 10 bps (to 49 bps and 9 bps, respectively), both of them statistically significant at the 99% level.

To further test the results, we run the model using the $25K-$10K MMDA spread. Under our hypothesis, the $100K-$25K MMDA spreads reflect something about the riskiness of the depository institution. Following similar reasoning, running the baseline analysis with the $25K-$10K MMDA spread would be expected to yield no large-bank pricing advantage. Consistent with that logic, we obtain an insignificant 8 bps pricing discrepancy in the opposite direction and report results in column (11) of Table 6.

We attempt to disassociate the large-bank advantage from other size benefits (such as economies of scale) by including size as an alternative regressor in the panel analysis. In particular, it may be the case that the true relationship is between premium and size and that the *Large* variable is simply acting as a proxy for size. If this were the case, then size would likely be significant when included in the analysis. However, the results given in column (12) show that this is not the case. Namely, the size variable is not statistically significant in the panel analysis and has the opposite sign from what would be predicted. This finding supports the view that the baseline results do not reflect simply generic benefits associated with increased size.

Smaller banks are sometimes thought to operate with entirely different business models from the ones used by even moderately sized banks. To ensure that our result is not being driven by the smallest banks, we run the analysis eliminating all banks in our sample below $1 billion. The results from column (13) establish a remaining 29 basis point discrepancy between this subset of banks and those above $200 billion. Thus, the main results are not driven by the smallest banks.

In the baseline analysis, we tried to remain fairly parsimonious and chose variables to reflect individual CAMELS components. Column (14) reports results using one of the many specifications considered that included alternative financial reporting data. In particular, this specification includes loan portfolio data intended to capture some of the ex post riskier exposures that banks held, namely, Construction and Development (CD), Commercial Real Estate (CRE), and Commercial and Industrial (CI) portfolios. Furthermore, to account for the seniority of uninsured depositors, this specification also includes a measure of all subordinated claims to assets (SubDebt) and a measure of uninsured deposits to assets (UnIns). Finally, it may be the case that large banks tend to offer products (wealth management, for instance) that affect the pricing behavior for large deposits. As a proxy for that possibility, the specification in column (14) also includes fee income from investment banking and fiduciary investment activities (Fee). The estimate with these added variables remains both statistically significant at 99% and economically significant at 34 bps.

As with the MSA fixed effects in column (15), we further test for geographical dependence by examining the deposit rates at banks for the same products in the same market-specifically, New York City. The New York City MSA is a particularly ideal candidate for this analysis for many reasons. Among them, it is the largest MSA in terms of population and it has a large number and wide variety of banks. With zero premium banks allowed into the analysis,[26] the data include 39 different banks, four of which have more than $200 billion: CitiGroup, Bank of America, JP Morgan Chase, and Wachovia. Reported in column (15), we find economically and statistically significant differences-of 100 bps-in the risk premium among retail deposits in the New York City market alone. These differences suggest that geographical differences are not driving the overall result. In unreported results, we conducted a similar analysis of each of the remaining four of the five largest metro areas: Los Angeles, Chicago, Dallas, and

---

[26]Ignoring zeros the result is even larger and significant, but forces the exclusion of one large bank which always posts a zero premium in the New York City MSA during the sample.

Philadelphia. In four of the five metro areas, the results hold, Chicago being the exception.

In columns (16) and (17), we report the panel results using the baseline analysis but adjusting the definition of Large, using definitions of $100 billion and $10 billion, respectively. Partially consistent with our interpretation, the large-bank discount rises as we increase the threshold. As should be expected, the estimate with $100 billion reported in column (16) is also significant, though lower than the baseline and between the estimate from the $10 billion and $200 billion specifications. Indeed, those banks larger than $200 billion entirely drive the differences between the $10 billion and the $100 billion definitions, as was seen in the cross-sectional analysis.

However, the 21 bps large-bank discount for $10 billion reported in column (17) is more problematic for interpreting the estimate as being the consequence of implicit government support. Precedent and common perception do not suggest that banks at this threshold would receive any extraordinary support.[27] Nevertheless, even if these 21 bps are the result of size-related risk benefits not captured by the other controls, the estimates suggest a remaining 18 bps discrepancy between the $10 billion banks and the banks greater than $200 billion. As the literature has often found that banks up to at least $10 billion exhibit economies of scale, this differential could be the consequence of such asset size benefits. Given the seniority of uninsured depositors, such a difference would still constitute a much larger funding advantage for subordinated claims. Furthermore, column (18) suggests that the differences between $10 billion banks and others may not be attributable to economies of scale. In that specification, we examine $10 billion institutions after the increase in the SMDIA and show that the systematic differences between these institutions and smaller ones remain. This is in contrast to $200 billion banks, whose sharp fall in risk premiums coincides with the higher insurance limits. Regardless, the analysis suggests that $200 billion and $10 billion banks behave differently.

---

[27]For example, uninsured depositors took losses at IndyMac in July 2008.

Column (19) reflects a check on the exclusion, under the baseline specification, of banks that always pay a zero premium. When we encompass all banks in the baseline specification, including those that always post a zero premium, the magnitude of the large-bank discount estimate falls slightly relative to that of the baseline specification, but remains statistically significant at 99% and economically significant at 27 bps. Finally, column (20) extends the baseline specification back to 2006, where the result remains comparable to the baseline. However, from the cross-sectional results, there is no compelling evidence on whether the price differences indeed predate the onset of the financial crisis.

7 Conclusion

This paper provides evidence that the largest banks pay significantly less on comparable deposits than their smaller bank counterparts. We demonstrate that this pricing advantage holds for both insured and uninsured deposit products. An implication of this first finding is that at least some of the funding advantage enjoyed by the largest banks is unrelated to government support by TBTF policies. Our second finding is that when we use a differencing approach in order to remove many non-risk components potentially embedded in deposit rates, large banks have a risk premium advantage. Finally, even after controlling for common balance-sheet measures of risk, we show that on risky deposits, the largest banks receive an economically and statistically significant discount of around 40 bps.

Each of these three findings is consistent with a TBTF subsidy paid to large banks. As is unavoidable with any analysis of TBTF, the difference in risk premiums is not necessarily a byproduct of TBTF policies. Indeed, it would be impossible to eliminate all *possible* alternatives. However, the difference remains even after eliminating many non-risk-based bank characteristics through the differencing approach, accounting for many standard risk measures, and a battery of robustness checks.

References

ACHARYA, V. V., D. ANGINER, AND A. J. WARBURTON (2013): "The End of Market Discipline? Investor Expectations of Implicit State Guarantees," SSRN eLibrary.

ACHARYA, V. V., AND N. MORA (2011): "Are Banks Passive Liquidity Backstops: Deposit Rates and Flows during the 2007-09 Crisis," NYU Stern, Working Paper.

ANDERSON, R. G., AND R. H. RASCHE (2001): "Retail Sweep Programs and Bank Reserves: 1994-1999," Federal Reserve Bank of St. Louis Review, 83, 51–72.

BAKER, D., AND T. MCARTHUR (2009): "The Value of the "Too Big to Fail" Big Bank Subsidy," CEPR Reports and Issue Briefs.

BEN-DAVID, I., A. PALVIA, AND C. SPATT (2011): "Bank De-Leveraging and the Limits to Market Discipline," Available at SSRN 2021505.

BERNANKE, B. S. (2009): in The Supervisory Capital Assessment ProgramJekyll Island, Georgia. Federal Reserve Bank of Atlanta 2009 Financial Markets Conference.

BREWER, ELIJAH, I., AND J. JAGTIANI (2013): "How Much Did Banks Pay to Become Too-Big-To-Fail and to Become Systemically Important?," Journal of Financial Services Research, 43(1), 1–35.

GANDHI, P., AND H. LUSTIG (2010): "Size Anomalies in U.S. Bank Stock Returns: A Fiscal Explanation," Working Paper 16553, National Bureau of Economic Research.

HEITFIELD, E., AND T. SABARWAL (2004): "What Drives Default and Prepayment on Subprime Auto Loans?," Journal of Real Estate Finance and Economics, 29(4), 457–477.

HERRING, R. J. (2002): "International Financial Conglomerates: Implications for Bank Insolvency Regimes," in Policy Challenges for the Financial Sector in the Context of

Globalization, Proceedings of the Second Annual Policy Seminar for Deputy Central Bank Governors.

HOVAKIMIAN, A., E. J. KANE, AND L. LAEVEN (2012): "Variation in Systemic Risk at US Banks During 1974-2010," Working Paper 18043, National Bureau of Economic Research.

IMAI, M. (2006): "Market Discipline and Deposit Insurance Reform in Japan," Journal of Banking & Finance, 30(12), 3433–3452.

KANE, E. J. (2000): "Incentives for Banking Megamergers: What Motives Might Regulators Infer from Event-Study Evidence?," Journal of Money, Credit and Banking, 32(3), pp.671–701.

——— (2009): "Extracting Nontransparent Safety Net Subsidies by Strategically Expanding and Contracting a Financial Institution's Accounting Balance Sheet," Journal of Financial Services Research, 36(2-3), 161–168.

KENNICKELL, A. B., M. L. KWAST, AND M. STARR-MCCLUER (1996): "Households' Deposit Insurance Coverage: Evidence and Analysis of Potential Reforms," Journal of Money, Credit and Banking, 28(3), pp.311–322.

KRISHNAKUMAR, J. (2006): Time Invariant Variables and Panel Data Models: A Generalised Frisch-Waugh Theorem and its Implications, Contributions to Economic Analysis. North-Holland (Elsevier Science), Amsterdam.

LI, Z., S. QU, AND J. ZHANG (2011): "Quantifying the Value of Implicit Government Guarantees for Large Financial Institutions," Modeling Methodology, Moody's Analytics.

NOSS, J., AND R. SOWERBUTTS (2012): "The Implicit Subsidy of Banks," SSRN eLibrary.

OAXACA, R. L., AND I. GEISLER (2003): "Fixed Effects Models with Time Invariant Variables: A Theoretical Note," Economics Letters, 80(3), 373 – 377.

O'HARA, M., AND W. SHAW (1990): "Deposit Insurance and Wealth Effects: The Value of Being "Too Big to Fail"," The Journal of Finance, 45(5), pp.1587–1600.

PARK, K., AND G. PENNACCHI (2009): "Harming Depositors and Helping Borrowers: The Disparate Impact of Bank Consolidation," Review of Financial Studies, 22(1), pp.1–40.

PENAS, M. F., AND H. ÜNAL (2004): "Gains in Bank Mergers: Evidence from the Bond Markets," Journal of Financial Economics, 74(1), 149–179.

POLACHEK, S. W., AND M.-K. KIM (1994): "Panel Estimates of the Gender Earnings Gap: Individual-specific Intercept and Individual-specific Slope Models," Journal of Econometrics, 61(1), 23 – 42.

SCHWEIKHARD, F., AND Z. TSESMELIDAKIS (2012): "The Impact of Government Interventions on CDS and Equity Markets," Available at SSRN: http://ssrn.com/abstract=1573377.

UEDA, K., AND B. W. DI MAURO (2012): "Quantifying Structural Subsidy Values for Systemically Important Financial Institutions," IMF Working Paper, (128).

VANHOOSE, D. D., AND D. B. HUMPHREY (2001): "Sweep Accounts, Reserve Management, and Interest Rate Volatility," Journal of Economics and Business, 53(4), 387–404.

Table 1: Control Variable Definitions

Abbreviation	Description (ratios)
Eq	Equity divided by total assets
NP	Loans which are 60-90 days overdue or in non-accrual status divided by total assets
LLR	Loan-loss reserves divided by total assets
Gr	Merger adjusted asset growth top coded at 100% and bottom coded at -50%
GrVol	8 quarter backward looking variance of asset growth
Inc	Before tax income divided by total assets
LiqAs	Sum of cash, treasuries, and GSE debt divided by total assets
Trad	Trading assets plus trading liabilities divided by total assets
InsDep	Insured deposits less insured brokered deposits divided by total assets
LIQ	$25K MMDA rate less the $10K MMDA rate
CD	Construction and Development loans divided by total assets
CI	Commercial and Industrial loans divided by total assets
CRE	Commercial Real Estate loans divided by total assets
SubDebt	Total assets less deposits and secured funding divided by total assets
Fee	Fiduciary and investment banking fees divided by total assets
UnIns	Uninsured deposits divided by total assets
Large	Dummy equal to 1 if assets exceed $200bn in 2008 dollars and 0 otherwise

Table 2: List of Big banks

Bank size is the aggregation of a banking institution to the regulatory high holder (i.e. files a Call Report). A bank is called Large in our baseline specification if its consolidated holding company has greater than $200 billion of assets in 2008 dollars. A '2' indicates the bank greater than $200bn and is in our sample, '1' indicates the bank greater than $100bn and is in our sample (though is not Large in the baseline), a '0' indicates the bank is greater than $100bn and is not in our sample, and an empty cell indicates the bank is smaller than $100bn. American Express, Countrywide, Goldman Sachs, MetLife, and Morgan Stanley are all bank holding companies which exceeded $100 billion in assets at some point during the sample period. However, none appear in our sample, likely because their retail deposit banking operations represent a relatively small portion of their activities. Of banks with significant retail components, only Washington Mutual is larger than our $200bn threshold and not present in the data. Our baseline definition also excluded US Bancorp, which is greater than the $200bn threshold but always posts a zero premium. AL=Ally; BA=Bank of America; BBT=BB&T; BNY=Bank of New York; C1=Capital One; CT=Citigroup; F3=Fifth Third; JP=JP Morgan; KC=KeyCorp; NC=National City; R=Regions; SS=State Street; ST=SunTrust; US=US Bancorp; WA=Wachovia; WF=Wells Fargo; WM=Washington Mutual; WSB=World Savings Bank.

Date	AL	BA	BBT	BNY	C1	CT	F3	JP	KC	NC	PNC	R	SS	ST	US	WA	WF	WM	WS	TOTAL
05-03-31	.	2	1	1	.	2	1	2	1	1	.	.	0	1	2	2	2	0	0	12
05-06-30	.	2	1	1	.	2	1	2	1	1	1	.	0	1	2	2	2	0	0	13
05-09-30	.	2	1	1	.	2	1	2	1	1	1	.	0	1	2	2	2	0	0	13
05-12-31	.	2	1	1	.	2	1	2	1	1	1	.	0	1	2	2	2	0	0	13
06-03-31	.	2	1	1	.	2	1	2	1	1	1	.	0	1	2	2	2	0	0	13
06-06-30	.	2	1	1	.	2	1	2	1	1	1	.	0	1	2	2	2	0	0	13
06-09-30	.	2	1	1	1	2	1	2	1	1	1	.	0	1	2	2	2	0	0	14
06-12-31	.	2	1	0	1	2	1	2	.	1	1	.	0	1	2	2	2	0	.	13
07-03-31	.	2	1	0	1	2	1	2	.	1	1	1	0	1	2	2	2	0	.	13
07-06-30	.	2	1	0	1	2	1	2	.	1	1	1	0	1	2	2	2	0	.	13
07-09-30	.	2	1	1	1	2	1	2	1	1	1	1	0	1	2	2	2	0	.	15
07-12-31	.	2	1	2	1	2	1	2	1	1	1	0	0	1	2	2	2	0	.	14
08-03-31	.	2	1	2	1	2	1	2	1	1	1	1	0	1	2	2	2	0	.	15
08-06-30	.	2	1	2	1	2	1	2	1	1	1	1	0	1	2	2	2	0	.	15
08-09-30	.	2	1	2	1	2	1	2	1	1	1	1	0	1	2	2	2	0	.	15
08-12-31	.	2	1	2	1	2	1	2	1	.	2	1	0	1	2	2	2	.	.	13
09-03-31	1	2	1	2	1	2	1	2	.	.	2	1	0	1	2	2	2	.	.	13
09-06-30	1	2	1	2	1	2	1	2	.	.	2	1	0	1	2	2	2	.	.	13
09-09-30	1	2	1	2	1	2	1	2	.	.	2	1	0	1	2	2	2	.	.	13
09-12-31	1	2	1	2	1	2	1	2	.	.	2	1	0	1	2	2	2	.	.	13
10-03-31	1	2	1	0	1	2	1	2	.	.	2	1	0	1	2	2	2	.	.	12
10-06-30	1	2	1	0	1	2	1	2	.	.	2	1	0	0	2	2	2	.	.	11
10-09-30	1	2	1	0	1	2	1	2	.	.	2	1	0	0	2	2	2	.	.	11

Table 3: Descriptive Statistics

This table provides the mean, standard deviation, and 5th and 95th percentiles of the sample for each variable. *Large* refers to banks more than $200 billion in consolidated depository institution assets.

Variable	Mean		Standard Deviation		5%		95%	
	Other	Large	Other	Large	Other	Large	Other	Large
Asset Volatility	0.0058	0.0222	0.0219	0.0422	0.0002	0.0006	0.0209	0.1288
CRE Loans	0.1912	0.0360	0.0992	0.0264	0.0430	0.0054	0.3659	0.0776
C&D Loans	0.1032	0.0173	0.0898	0.0130	0.0062	0.0014	0.2853	0.0355
C&I Loans	0.0988	0.1023	0.0674	0.0251	0.0150	0.0706	0.2240	0.1604
Equity	0.0970	0.0943	0.0395	0.0126	0.0621	0.0754	0.1498	0.1167
Fee Income	0.0002	0.0007	0.0012	0.0003	0.0000	0.0003	0.0009	0.0014
Growth	0.0231	0.0361	0.0790	0.1386	-0.0510	-0.0487	0.1203	0.0949
Income	0.0008	0.0026	0.0068	0.0030	-0.0096	-0.0046	0.0056	0.0058
Insured Deposits	0.5459	0.2386	0.1612	0.1264	0.2583	0.0616	0.7838	0.4469
Liquid Assets	0.1250	0.1131	0.0927	0.0647	0.0236	0.0382	0.2970	0.2310
Liquidity Premium	0.2194	0.2106	0.3140	0.3508	0.0000	0.0000	0.7800	1.0520
Loan Loss Reserves	0.0103	0.0113	0.0064	0.0066	0.0039	0.0051	0.0225	0.0245
Non-Performing	0.0217	0.0160	0.0333	0.0144	0.0001	0.0028	0.0841	0.0439
Risk Premium	0.3894	0.1634	0.3675	0.2430	0.0000	0.0000	1.0100	0.7128
Subordinated Debt	0.1171	0.4230	0.0738	0.1420	0.0082	0.2163	0.2198	0.6878
Trading Assets	0.0008	0.1212	0.0073	0.0908	0.0000	0.0146	0.0002	0.2788
Uninsured Deposits	0.1880	0.1875	0.1090	0.0530	0.0399	0.0893	0.3954	0.2558
$100K MMDA	1.5948	1.2205	1.0391	1.0537	0.3500	0.0100	3.7500	3.8835
$10K MMDA	0.9834	0.8338	0.7790	0.6342	0.1500	0.0100	2.5000	2.3109
$25K MMDA	1.2033	1.0445	0.8832	0.9158	0.2112	0.0100	3.0000	2.9760

Table 4: Cross Sectional Regressions Premium

Results from OLS cross sectional regressions for 2005 Q1 through 2010 Q2. The independent variable is risk premium and the variable of interest is Large. The risk premium is defined as the branch level difference in the $100K MMDA rate and the $25K MMDA rate aggregated to the regulatory high holder. Each regression excludes banks that always post a zero premium and uses a *Large* threshold of $200 billion. Variables definitions appear in Table 1. N is the number of banks. Reporting robust standard errors.

Date	Large	Liq	Eq	Gr	NP	LLR	Inc	GrVol	Ins	LiqAs	Trad	R^2	N
05-03-31	0.0708 (0.1083)	0.0601 (0.0589)	-0.6503** (0.3239)	-0.1734 (0.1675)	1.1177 (2.0153)	0.5138 (3.8926)	-11.273** (4.9826)	0.9135* (0.4897)	0.0225 (0.0805)	0.1568 (0.1399)	-1.2868** (0.5736)	0.0229	720
05-06-30	0.0140 (0.0988)	0.0831 (0.0544)	-0.4043 (0.4830)	0.1517 (0.1242)	-1.8551 (1.5731)	2.9052 (4.2163)	-8.9953* (4.5874)	0.8216 (0.6708)	-0.0280 (0.0882)	0.2769* (0.1640)	-1.3706** (0.6050)	0.0269	784
05-09-30	-0.0438 (0.1219)	0.0084 (0.0486)	-0.0432 (0.4451)	0.0104 (0.1714)	-1.5157 (1.7495)	4.1205 (4.7687)	-8.6351 (6.3163)	1.1489 (0.8490)	-0.0965 (0.0984)	0.1508 (0.1719)	-1.4206* (0.7677)	0.0134	832
05-12-31	0.0792 (0.2223)	0.0613 (0.0449)	-0.7259* (0.4283)	0.0579 (0.2096)	-1.8434 (1.7855)	3.4633 (4.8348)	-10.237 (7.3139)	0.8197 (0.6487)	-0.1244 (0.1021)	0.2397 (0.1643)	-1.8338* (0.9460)	0.0153	882
06-03-31	-0.1091 (0.2554)	0.0608 (0.0376)	-0.4378 (0.4613)	0.0410 (0.2619)	-0.3103 (1.7669)	-4.9480 (5.6752)	-10.736 (8.0854)	-0.3218 (0.6278)	-0.2064** (0.0939)	0.1855 (0.1607)	-0.6531 (1.6134)	0.0142	920
06-06-30	-0.0274 (0.2791)	0.0299 (0.0346)	-0.5706 (0.4161)	0.3129 (0.1975)	-2.5291 (2.0960)	1.1310 (5.7767)	-6.5821 (9.4912)	-1.0965 (0.7616)	-0.1801* (0.1007)	0.4929*** (0.1812)	-1.1959 (1.6571)	0.0186	973
06-09-30	-0.1036 (0.2686)	0.0249 (0.0322)	-0.0666 (0.3856)	0.4403** (0.1841)	-1.6983 (2.0427)	0.8541 (5.9734)	-16.307** (6.5541)	-1.2700 (0.8422)	-0.0077 (0.1112)	0.4249** (0.1720)	-0.4336 (0.7000)	0.0321	974
06-12-31	-0.3775* (0.2208)	0.0548 (0.0345)	-0.3682 (0.3775)	0.2945 (0.2951)	-1.6573 (2.0752)	-4.1458 (5.8414)	-6.2314* (3.7751)	-0.3069 (0.7233)	0.0237 (0.1136)	0.3413* (0.1750)	-0.2088 (1.4153)	0.0187	976
07-03-31	-0.5687*** (0.1770)	0.0616* (0.0337)	0.0440 (0.2852)	-0.0798 (0.1729)	-0.7228 (1.9750)	2.8355 (6.0498)	-8.3958 (6.1611)	-0.4276 (0.5134)	-0.0234 (0.1165)	0.3596** (0.1644)	1.1741 (1.0451)	0.0169	1,002
07-06-30	-0.5333** (0.2163)	0.0661* (0.0348)	-0.3382 (0.3810)	-0.1158 (0.1484)	-1.3515 (1.6701)	-0.9836 (6.0196)	0.9867 (3.1605)	-0.0265 (0.4483)	-0.0692 (0.1091)	0.4890*** (0.1867)	0.8190 (1.1887)	0.0166	1,011
07-09-30	-0.4443** (0.2020)	0.0671* (0.0348)	-0.5197* (0.2782)	-0.1386 (0.2013)	-1.6467 (1.4812)	-1.8116 (5.5045)	-0.8878 (3.1050)	0.5502 (0.3498)	-0.0588 (0.0979)	0.5661*** (0.1898)	0.0484 (1.0567)	0.0214	1,020
07-12-31	-0.3496* (0.1885)	0.0492 (0.0356)	-0.8410*** (0.2738)	0.0708 (0.1369)	-1.3944 (1.1181)	-5.3422 (4.7324)	-3.6809 (2.6731)	-0.3750 (0.4169)	0.0286 (0.0929)	0.3795** (0.1703)	-0.2515 (0.9968)	0.0205	999
08-03-31	-0.1708 (0.1873)	0.0376 (0.0400)	-0.4012 (0.3468)	0.0718 (0.1463)	-1.2990** (0.6046)	-3.9696 (3.2832)	-7.3563** (3.6638)	0.2960 (0.5888)	0.1028 (0.0765)	0.0741 (0.1268)	-0.5549 (0.8116)	0.0154	1,014
08-06-30	-0.2892* (0.1657)	0.0427 (0.0391)	-0.3430 (0.3065)	0.0834 (0.1363)	-0.1358 (0.4773)	-5.7132* (2.5800)	-1.6418 (2.1184)	0.4986 (0.6585)	0.0378 (0.0782)	0.0539 (0.1259)	-0.1816 (0.8940)	0.0145	1,008
08-09-30	-0.0564 (0.1647)	0.0767* (0.0414)	-0.3051 (0.2682)	0.1698 (0.1266)	-0.5028 (0.4739)	-4.0641 (2.3781)	-2.3621* (1.0998)	-0.1280 (0.4602)	0.0435 (0.0832)	0.0028 (0.1326)	-1.7104** (0.8346)	0.0188	1,003
08-12-31	0.0197 (0.1264)	0.0399 (0.0379)	-0.1508 (0.2002)	0.0507 (0.1100)	0.5899 (0.3305)	-7.6879*** (1.8948)	-0.5697 (1.0820)	0.1866 (0.3667)	0.0247 (0.0596)	-0.0594 (0.1077)	-1.9183** (0.6871)	0.0205	1,350
09-03-31	0.0127 (0.0925)	0.0844** (0.0444)	-0.0841 (0.1911)	0.2459** (0.1223)	0.6439** (0.2677)	-5.4688*** (1.5606)	-0.0494 (1.3294)	0.1427 (0.2799)	0.0289 (0.0565)	-0.0325 (0.0927)	-1.7399*** (0.6744)	0.0268	1,374
09-06-30	-0.0180 (0.1011)	0.1462*** (0.0506)	0.0749 (0.1856)	0.2096 (0.1310)	0.3257 (0.2186)	-4.2451*** (1.2316)	-1.0710 (1.0525)	0.4636 (0.3422)	0.0574 (0.0533)	0.0169 (0.0855)	-1.6060** (0.8116)	0.0332	1,465
09-09-30	-0.0010 (0.0989)	0.0975** (0.0445)	0.0436 (0.1508)	0.0636 (0.0702)	0.2949 (0.1926)	-3.2682*** (1.1149)	-2.0109 (1.2543)	0.5467** (0.2609)	0.0996** (0.0450)	-0.0730 (0.0660)	-1.2543* (0.6781)	0.0212	1,652
09-12-31	0.0430 (0.0867)	0.1336*** (0.0416)	-0.0175 (0.1600)	0.1419* (0.0606)	-0.0534 (0.1604)	-1.7312* (0.7829)	-1.7796** (0.8411)	0.1352 (0.2718)	0.1132*** (0.0434)	-0.0992 (0.0635)	-1.5824** (0.6612)	0.0246	1,717
10-03-31	-0.0571 (0.0666)	0.1728*** (0.0422)	-0.0470 (0.1695)	0.0677 (0.0831)	-0.0293 (0.1415)	-2.6757*** (0.7530)	-4.1414*** (1.2715)	0.4073 (0.2779)	0.1063*** (0.0409)	-0.0391 (0.0601)	-0.9353* (0.4854)	0.0327	1,773
10-06-30	-0.0702 (0.0678)	0.1707*** (0.0391)	-0.2113 (0.1688)	0.0657 (0.0826)	0.1173 (0.1410)	-1.4192** (0.6200)	-0.1914 (0.3655)	0.4555 (0.2865)	0.0971*** (0.0374)	0.0093 (0.0550)	-0.9243* (0.5280)	0.0256	1,872
10-09-30	0.0001 (0.0627)	0.1532*** (0.0405)	-0.0174 (0.1662)	0.0069 (0.0821)	0.0421 (0.1427)	-1.4425** (0.7014)	-1.7171* (1.0091)	0.0826 (0.2120)	0.1025*** (0.0371)	-0.0489 (0.0509)	-1.1315** (0.4855)	0.0262	1,765

* significant at 10%, ** significant at 5%, and *** significant at 1%

Table 5: Panel Regression Results, Alternative Specifications (1) through (10)

Results from a panel regression of the risk premium on risk variables, with a decomposition of errors by a Large dummy. Risk premium is defined as the branch-level difference in the $100K MMDA rate and the $25K MMDA rate aggregated to the regulatory high holder. The baseline estimation appears in Column (1) and uses data from 2007 Q1, until 2008 Q2, inclusive. It excludes banks that always post a zero premium, and it uses a TBTF threshold of $200 billion. Column (2) reports results estimated after the policy change, 2008 Q4 to 2010 Q2. Column (3) reports fixed effects estimates. All other columns use these criteria unless noted otherwise. Column (4) reports estimates using Random Effects. Column (5) reports estimates using a Pooled Estimate. Column (6) reports estimates using a Pooled Estimate after the policy change. Column (7) reports estimates fixing the set of banks to those in the sample at 2007 Q1. Column (8) reports estimates fixing the set of banks to those in the sample at 2007 Q1 after the policy change. Column (9) reports estimates aggregating branches to the bank-MSA level and controls for MSA fixed effects. Column (10) reports estimates aggregating branches to the bank-MSA level and controls for MSA fixed effects after the policy change. Definitions of variables appear in Table 1.

Variable	(1)	(2)	(3)	(4)	(5)	(6)	(7)	(8)	(9)	(10)
Large	-0.388***	-0.035	-0.403***	-0.004	-0.432**	0.023	-0.387***	-0.186***	-0.492***	-0.091***
	(0.112)	(0.039)	(0.156)	(0.088)	(0.196)	(0.068)	(0.112)	(0.043)	(0.087)	(0.026)
Liq	-0.019	-0.049	-0.004	-0.020	0.048	0.098***	0.032	0.071	0.049	0.033
	(0.045)	(0.034)	(0.039)	(0.032)	(0.031)	(0.035)	(0.055)	(0.051)	(0.041)	(0.057)
Eq	-0.146	-0.149	-0.225	-0.131	-0.350	-0.151	1.340	-0.320	-0.096	-0.044
	(0.331)	(0.169)	(0.214)	(0.133)	(0.244)	(0.134)	(0.907)	(0.356)	(0.258)	(0.199)
Gr	0.040	0.078**	0.014	0.102***	-0.018	0.262***	0.074	0.098	-0.061	0.086*
	(0.078)	(0.036)	(0.068)	(0.034)	(0.113)	(0.058)	(0.104)	(0.062)	(0.100)	(0.046)
NP	-0.003	-0.066	-0.100	0.008	-0.597	0.243*	0.544	-0.157	-0.723	-0.069
	(0.456)	(0.155)	(0.403)	(0.108)	(0.600)	(0.125)	(0.444)	(0.263)	(0.646)	(0.226)
LLR	2.258	-0.827	0.924	-1.268**	-2.756	-2.826***	1.000	0.207	4.655	0.199
	(2.315)	(0.631)	(2.035)	(0.518)	(3.909)	(0.637)	(2.349)	(0.903)	(4.212)	(0.875)
Inc	0.071	-0.060	-0.083	-0.171	-1.148	-1.042**	-0.671	0.370	-0.646	0.173
	(0.900)	(0.270)	(0.839)	(0.267)	(1.990)	(0.481)	(0.944)	(0.330)	(0.950)	(0.385)
GrVol	0.773	0.391	0.537	0.478*	0.052	0.739**	0.247	-1.256**	0.707	0.342
	(0.539)	(0.303)	(0.457)	(0.277)	(0.501)	(0.344)	(1.256)	(0.503)	(0.482)	(0.322)
Ins	-0.084	0.000	-0.054	0.033	-0.068	0.083**	0.006	-0.033	0.000	-0.023
	(0.127)	(0.045)	(0.074)	(0.033)	(0.084)	(0.038)	(0.123)	(0.070)	(0.138)	(0.058)
LiqAs	0.192	0.023	0.223*	0.007	0.292*	-0.062	0.371*	0.010	0.184	0.067
	(0.168)	(0.063)	(0.118)	(0.048)	(0.154)	(0.059)	(0.199)	(0.081)	(0.220)	(0.092)
Trad	0.000	-1.519	0.122	-1.660**	0.208	-1.493***	0.217	-0.010	0.797	-1.006
	(0.594)	(0.971)	(0.582)	(0.694)	(0.949)	(0.499)	(0.633)	(0.856)	(0.575)	(0.793)
N	904	1,678	904	1,670	904	1,670	625	549	926	1,691
Rsq	0.803	0.779	0.067	0.102	0.031	0.049	0.812	0.799	0.114	0.125
Time FE	YES	YES	YES	YES	YES	YES	YES	YES	YES	YES
MSA FE	NO	NO	NO	NO	NO	NO	NO	NO	YES	YES

* significant at 10%, ** significant at 5%, and *** significant at 1%.

41

Table 6: Panel Regression Results, Alternative Specifications (11) through (20)

Results from a panel regression of the risk premium on risk variables, with a decomposition of errors by a Large dummy. Risk premium is defined as the branch-level difference in the $100K MMDA rate and the $25K MMDA rate aggregated to the regulatory high holder. All other columns use these criteria from the baseline except as noted. Column (11) reports estimates using the $25K - 10K$ spread as the dependent variable. Column (12) reports estimates from a panel FE estimation with size as a time varying control variable. Column (13) reports estimates using only those banks larger than $1 billion. Column (14) includes additional risk measures associated with the crisis (CD, CI, and CRE concentrations), measures for priority of claims relative to uninsured deposits (SubDebt, Unins), and a proxy for the presence of wealth management services for large depositors (Fee). Column (15) includes only branches in the New York City MSA and includes banks that post only a zero risk premium. Column (16) reports estimates using a Large threshold of $100 billion. Column (17) reports estimates using a Large threshold of $10 billion. Column (18) reports estimates using a Large threshold of $10 billion after the policy change. Column (19) includes all banks, including those that always post a zero risk premium. Column (20) reports estimates using 2006 Q1, until 2008 Q2, inclusive. Definitions of variables appear in Table 1.

Variable	(11)	(12)	(13)	(14)	(15)	(16)	(17)	(18)	(19)	(20)
Large	0.283		-0.294***	-0.338***	-1.057***	-0.283***	-0.214***	-0.147***	-0.267***	-0.356***
	(0.247)		(0.110)	(0.111)	(0.141)	(0.069)	(0.050)	(0.020)	(0.094)	(0.107)
Size		0.032								
		(0.076)								
Liq	-0.196	-0.018	0.022	-0.018	0.115	-0.019	-0.019	-0.049	-0.004	0.013
	(0.181)	(0.045)	(0.088)	(0.045)	(0.237)	(0.045)	(0.045)	(0.035)	(0.040)	(0.039)
Eq	-0.586	-0.048	0.712	-0.034	3.621	-0.146	-0.146	-0.153	-0.075	0.202
	(0.536)	(0.435)	(1.533)	(0.533)	(3.195)	(0.331)	(0.331)	(0.169)	(0.296)	(0.231)
NP		0.021	0.149	0.043	3.019	-0.003	-0.003	-0.065	-0.110	0.328
		(0.454)	(1.061)	(0.466)	(4.083)	(0.456)	(0.456)	(0.155)	(0.358)	(0.417)
LLR	0.193	2.418	5.575	2.100	10.281	2.258	2.258	-0.859	1.462	0.455
	(2.862)	(2.397)	(4.446)	(2.316)	(20.362)	(2.315)	(2.315)	(0.637)	(1.688)	(2.561)
Inc	-0.680	0.097	0.501	0.100	17.008	0.071	0.071	-0.064	0.350	-0.614
	(0.911)	(0.899)	(0.877)	(0.912)	(15.676)	(0.900)	(0.900)	(0.271)	(0.738)	(0.989)
GrVol	1.060***	0.796	1.516	0.827	4.154	0.773	0.773	0.385	0.567	0.533
	(0.409)	(0.531)	(1.663)	(0.525)	(5.348)	(0.539)	(0.539)	(0.303)	(0.458)	(0.500)
Ins	0.109	-0.079	0.230	-0.126	-2.092*	-0.084	-0.084	-0.001	-0.057	-0.145
	(0.187)	(0.126)	(0.221)	(0.183)	(1.154)	(0.127)	(0.127)	(0.045)	(0.108)	(0.089)
LiqAs	0.055	0.189	0.227	0.234	0.032	0.192	0.192	0.022	0.155	0.266**
	(0.153)	(0.169)	(0.445)	(0.190)	(0.316)	(0.168)	(0.168)	(0.063)	(0.120)	(0.131)
Trad	-1.488	-0.020	0.310	0.039	0.686	0.000	0.000	-1.523	-0.034	0.174
	(0.961)	(0.597)	(0.994)	(0.615)	(1.214)	(0.594)	(0.594)	(0.970)	(0.431)	(0.395)
CD				0.160						
				(0.349)						
CI				-0.020						
				(0.452)						
CRE				0.066						
				(0.322)						
Subdebt				-0.105						
				(0.370)						
DepUnins				-0.060						
				(0.205)						
N	904	904	255	904	39	904	904	1,670	1,224	1,029
Rsq	0.782	0.803	0.811	0.803	0.873	0.803	0.803	0.777	0.849	0.783
Time FE	YES	YES	YES	YES	YES	YES	YES	YES	YES	YES
MSA FE	NO	NO	NO	NO	NO	NO	NO	NO	NO	NO

* significant at 10%, ** significant at 5%, and *** significant at 1%.